Let's Talk
Cheyenne

An audio course

Ted Risingsun and Wayne Leman

auDIO·FORUM

A division of Jeffrey Norton Publishers, Inc.
Madison, Connecticut

Let's Talk Cheyenne

ISBN: 1-57970-092-6 text only
       1-57970-170-1 text and audio CDs
       1-57970-091-8 text and audio cassettes

Published by Audio-Forum,
a division of Jeffrey Norton Publishers, Inc.
One Orchard Park Road, Madison CT 06443

Printed in the United States of America.

Let's Talk Cheyenne

**Dedicated to the memory
of
Voestaa'e
Josephine Stands in Timber Glenmore
1920-1990**
*Wife, mother, grandmother,
great-grandmother, friend,
language teacher.
Gifted with hospitality and laughter.*

INTRODUCTION TO THE
CHEYENNE ALPHABET AND SOUNDS:

This booklet contains in printed form the contents of the two tapes in this basic Cheyenne language learning course. Cheyenne words are spelled with the 14 letters of the Cheyenne alphabet. Basically, this alphabet is the same as the one which was designed by the missionary linguist Rodolphe Petter in the late 1890's, with a small amount of upgrading due to progress which has been made in the scientific study of languages and alphabet systems. The Cheyenne alphabet was designed so that someone who already knows how to read English can begin to pronounce Cheyenne words fairly soon. Since the beginning of Federally-funded bilingual education programs among the Cheyenne people in the early 1970's, there has been new interest in reading, writing, and speaking the Cheyenne language.

There are 3 Cheyenne vowels: **a, e,** and **o.**
There are 11 consonants: **h, k, ', m, n, p, s, š, t, v,** and **x.**

Here is how the Cheyenne vowels are pronounced:

a sounds like 'a' as in English 'father.'
e usually sounds like a 'short-i' as in English 'hit.'
o sounds like a 'long-o' as in English 'note.'

In their standard pronunciation, the letters **h, m, n,** and **s** are pronounced in Cheyenne as they are in English.
The letter **'** is called a 'glottal stop' (or just 'glottal'). It is a very important letter in Cheyenne and is found in many words. It causes there to be a very quick stop in the sound of a vowel. The glottal stop sound can be heard in English separating the two syllables of the exclamation 'oh-oh.' The glottal stop is typed here with the apostrophe mark, **'**, but sometimes is written or typed with the upper part of a question mark, **?**. You will hear many glottal stops on these tapes. One of the words which you will hear which has a glottal stop is **he'e** meaning 'woman.'

The letters **k, p,** and **t** are pronounced softly in Cheyenne, in their standard pronunciation. This 'soft' (unaspirated) sound is exactly as these letters are pronounced in English when they follow the English letter **s**. Listen to the soft sound of these letters in these English words:

> skip
> spoon
> stick

Here are some Cheyenne words with the soft-sounding **k, p,** and **t**:

ka'éškóne	child
póéso	cat
hoestato	belt

This soft way of pronouncing these three Cheyenne letters is different from the 'aspirated' (or, 'hard') sound that these letters have in English when they begin a word, as in these English words:

> kite
> pony
> table

The letter **š** is called an 'esh,' or sometimes we call it a 'duck' since the Cheyenne word for 'duck' has two of these sounds, **šé'še.** The 'esh,' or 'duck,' sound is pronounced the same as the two English letters sh, as in the English word 'shirt.' In this booklet the 'esh' letter is printed as **š**, but in some other materials it is printed as **ꚃ**. The second form can be typed on any typewriter or computer by first typing the letter s, then backspacing and typing over it the double quotation mark, **"**. Both ways of writing this sound are just fine.

The Cheyenne letter **v** is sometimes pronounced much like the English letter v, as in the Cheyenne word **vee'e** 'dwelling or tepee.' At other times, especially when it comes before the **a** or **o** vowels, it sounds more like the English letter w, as in Cheyenne **váótséva** '(a single) deer.' If you listen to a Cheyenne person pronounce **váótséva**, you will also notice that the last **v** in the word sounds much like the English letter **f**. This is because it comes before a 'whispered' (voiceless) vowel at the end of a word.

The sound of the Cheyenne letter **x** is not found in English. It sounds something like the letter h, but has a harsher sound than h. The Cheyenne word for 'skunk' begins with this sound, **xãõ'o**. The technical name for this sound is voiceless velar fricative. It is a common sound in the German language, as in the German word Achtung!

Cheyenne vowels are often 'whispered' or voiceless. If you say just a single word, then the last vowel is always whispered. If you say a phrase or sentence, then the last vowel is whispered. Sometimes vowels which are not at the end of words are whispered, and when they are, we put a little mark over them to show that they are whispered. The mark can be either a dot or a small circle.

Here are some words with whispered vowels marked:

tåhpeno	flute
sémonôtse	boats
ého'êhneo'o	they are coming
éhávêséva'e	it's bad
émo'ôhtávo	it's black
môxe'êstoo'o	book, paper
måhpeva	in the water
kôsáne	goats, sheep (plural)
kåsováahe	young man
nåhtõtse	my pet (especially a horse)
nêstaévåhósevóomåtse	I'll see you later.

A Difficult Thing To Learn:

Probably the most difficult thing to learn when you are trying to speak or read Cheyenne is how to pronounce a consonant when it is followed by exactly these three kinds of letters: a vowel with a dot or circle over it, the letter **h**, then another vowel which is not whispered. The four letters in this sequence are called a 'complex syllable.' According to the underlying structure of the Cheyenne language these four letters are two syllables, but they are pronounced as a single phonetic syllable.

The first consonant takes on a 'hard' or 'aspirated' sound, instead of its standard sound. Here are some Cheyenne words with complex syllables. If you can, listen to a Cheyenne speaker pronounce these words. Some of them will also occur on the tapes, so you can also hear them as you listen to the tapes:

tôhohko	hammer
måhẽõ'o	house
påhoešestôtse	cradleboard
vôhe'so	nest
náhkôheo'o	bears (contrast the soft **k** in **nahkohe** bear)
nêhe'še	then
éamo'åhéotse	he ran by
ésôheo'o	tepee lining, dew cloth

Accent (Pitch) Marks:

By now you may have noticed accent marks on some of the Cheyenne words. These marks indicate different pitches or tones on Cheyenne vowels. The acute accent mark, ´, as in **á**, indicates high pitch, and ¯ or ~ or umlaut, as in **ã**, indicates a middle level pitch. If a vowel has no pitch mark, then it is pronounced with a low pitch or tone. Cheyenne tones are important; sometimes just a difference in tone (pitch) means you have two different words. For example, **hẽ'e**, with mid tone, means 'woman,' but **he'e**, with low tone, means 'liver.' In some Cheyenne printed material the mid tone is written with a straight line (macron) over a vowel. At other times, the mid tone is written with a wavy line (tilde) over a vowel, as in **hẽ'e**. There is no difference in pitch between these two ways of writing the mid pitch. (The preferred way of indicating mid pitch is with the straight line macron, but for some printers, it is easier to use the tilde.)

Well, are you ready to listen to the tapes now? Start with Tape #1, Side A. We often add comments in the booklet which are not on the tapes. These are meant to help you, but it can be confusing at first if you might expect the speaking on the tapes to be exactly as in the booklet. Go slowly, listen carefully, stop your recorder often, and practice what you hear. And take the time to read our extra comments in the booklet.

Tape 1-A

This tape (as well as Tape #2) teaches some basic Cheyenne. We will have Cheyenne words and phrases in different areas of life, like greetings, and when you go to visit someone. Listen carefully to the Cheyenne words as you hear them, and practice them, and then try to go out and practice speaking in a friendly way with Cheyenne people, and you will find that they appreciate your efforts to speak Cheyenne. don't worry about making mistakes; they will still appreciate that you are trying to learn Cheyenne.

(Important note: These tapes only introduce you to some of the basics of the Cheyenne language. There is much more to the Cheyenne language than what is found on these tapes. There are thousands of words in Cheyenne and we can only give a small percentage of them on these tapes. However, if you diligently practice what you hear on the tapes, you will have a good start at beginning to talk and understand Cheyenne.)

Greetings:
First we'll teach ways of saying a greeting:

'Good morning' is **påhávevóonā'o** (many people also say **pêhévevóonā'o**).
'Good day' is **påháveéšeeva** (or, **pêhéveéšeeva**).
   Epåháveéšeeve (or, **Epêhéveéšeeve**) means 'It is a good day.'
Another way of saying 'it is a good day' is **Epåhávatamáno'e**, or, **Epêhévatamáno'e**.

A word for 'Hi!' is **Haaahe**. That's only for men (to say).

Another common form of greeting is 'How are you?' **Népåhávomóhtåhehe?** (or, **Népêhévomóhtåhehe?**; both literally mean 'Are you feeling good?').

The answer would be **Héehe'e, nápåhávomóhtahe** (or **nápêhévomóhtahe**); (meaning, 'Yes, I'm feeling good.')

In the use of 'good,' like 'Good morning,' or, 'I feel good,' or just the word 'good,' we have two ways of saying the beginning of the word. And this is **-pêhéva'e** and **-påháva'e**. Those are two different ways of saying the same thing. (The older way of speaking, perhaps said mostly by some older men today, has the a vowel for 'good,' as **påháv**, while it seems that most Cheyennes today pronounce words with the meaning of 'good' in them with the e vowel, as **pêhév**. Notice that these words, or parts of words, have complex syllables, so the **p** will have an aspirated (hard) sound. For simplicity, and because words with the meaning 'good' in them are so common, we sometimes write the **p** without the complex syllable, which is easier to read, but proper pronunciation still requires the aspirated (hard) sound. For example, 'it is good' is technically **épêhéva'e**, but the simplified way of writing the same word is **épéva'e**. Cheyenne speakers themselves do not seem to need the help of the pitch marks for reading, so you may sometimes see 'it's good' written simply as **epeva'e**.)

Appreciation:

Here are some ways of expressing appreciation:

Thank you, **hahoo**. This is a word used by most Plains Indians.

For Cheyenne, specifically, 'thank you' is **néá'eše**. Or, **néá'ešemeno**, 'thank you'--**néá'ešemeno** means, in the plural, like, there's a group, meaning, 'we thank you,' **néá'ešemeno**. This is in talking either to a person or a group of persons.

Visiting:
And now some phrases about visiting:

'I've come visiting,' **náho'ėho'õhtse.** That is, 'I've come visiting,' and the next one would be: 'I'm (come) visiting you,' **ného'nåho'õhtsevåtse.**

The answer to 'coming to visit' would be **Epėhéva'e tséxho'ėhneto,** meaning 'it is good you came.'

Another way of saying 'I've come to visit,' **ného'héve'hoomåtse,** meaning 'I have come to see you.' **Náto'seévåhóó'óhtse** is 'I'm going back home.' 'I'll see you again' **nėstaévåhósevóomåtse.** 'Come again!' or 'Come again sometimes!' **né'évåhósėho'ėhneo'o.**

Weather:
Here are some phrases about the weather:

It's cold	**Etonéto.**
It's (very) hot	**Ehoháohõ'ta.**
It's raining	**Ehoo'kõho.**
It's snowing	**Eho'ééto.**

Another way of saying 'it's hot,' **Eháaehõ'ta.**

It's windy	**Eháá'ha,** or **Ehomóhtóná'ha.**
It's a cold wind	**Etonôhtã'ha.**
Is it cold?	**Etonétohe?**
Is it hot?	**Eháoho'tahe?**
Is it raining?	**Ehoo'kôhohe?**
Is it snowing?	**Eho'éetohe?**

Notice that the question is formed by adding the suffix **-he** to the end of the verb. We say that questions such as this which can be answered with 'yes' or 'no' are in the Interrogative mode in Cheyenne.

| It must have rained | móhoo'kôhóhanéhe. |
| It must have snowed | móho'éetôhanéhe. |

(Note: Verbs beginning with **mó-**, and taking negative suffixes, like the last two words, are in the Inferential mode. In Cheyenne, if you have not actually seen or experienced something yourself, you must shift the mode of the verb from the standard eye-witness mode, like **Eho'ééto** 'it's snowing' to some other mode. If you have figured something out from the evidence available to you, for example, if you walk outside and see some snow on the ground, but you hadn't actually seen the snow fall, then you would say **móho'éetôhanéhe** 'it must have snowed.' There are other verb modes in Cheyenne, also, such as the Attributive (or Hearsay) mode, for situations where you were told something by someone else, but did not actually see or experience it yourself, and the Preterit mode, where you are exclaiming about something (the Attributive and Preterit modes are also commonly used when telling Cheyenne legends). Cheyenne verb modes are further illustrated and explained in the reference grammar listed at the beginning of this booklet. Note, however, that in the grammar book the Inferential mode of Cheyenne is labeled Dubitative, and the Preterit mode is labeled Mediate.)

Eating and Drinking:

This next section is about eating and drinking:

Are you hungry?	Néháeanahe?
I am hungry	Náháeána.
I want to eat	Námésêhétáno.
I'm thirsty	Námanétáno (literally, 'I want to drink,'

depending upon the situation, today this can often imply wanting to drink alcohol, but it does not have to mean this, and it can be said for simply being thirsty).

Let's eat	Nétamésèhema!
Let's go eat	Nétåhémèsèhema! Nétåhémèsèhémáne!
Come eat!	Hémèseestse! or, to a group (plural),
	Hémèsehe!
Eat!	Méseestse!
Give me more!	Hosèstse néxhósèhoxomèstse!
	(literally, 'Some feed me more!')
Are you full?	Nééšená'so'enôhehe?
I'm full	Nééšená'so'enohe.
Hénáá'e tséméseto?	What are you eating?
I'm eating deer meat	Námese váotseváheho'évohkôtse,
	or, Námévo váótséva.

(Note: the difference between these two phrases is that the first has the verb **Námese** which requires an inanimate object, which **váotseváhe-ho'évohkôtse** is, while the verb **Námévo** requires an animate object, which **váótséva** is. The second phrase literally means 'I'm eating (a) deer.' In technical terms, the first verb is TI, meaning Transitive Inanimate, while the second verb is TA, meaning Transitive Animate. See the reference grammar (pages 17-18) of Cheyenne for further details about verb classification according to transitivity and gender (animacy) of the verb's object.)

I'm eating bread	**Námese kóhkonôheo'o.**
I'm eating berries	**Námésenôtse menôtse**

(Note: The verb is also inflected for the plurality of the object, **menôtse** 'berries.')

(The) meat tastes good	**Ho'évohkôtse épåháveéno'e**
	(or, **épèhéveéno'e**).
(The) berries taste good	**Menôtse épåháveéno'énèstse**
	(or, **épèhéveéno'énèstse**).
(Do) you want coffee?	**Mónèstsenomēne?** (Literally, 'Do

you want to drink something hot?' Coffee is implied.)

coffee	**mo'ôhtávèhohpe**
tea	**véhpotséhohpe**
soft drink	**toóomåšé'šestôtse**

Pass the salt!	**Né'asètanôtse vóhpoma'ôtse!**
Pass the pepper!	**Né'asètanôtse méhnemenôtse!**
Pass the sugar!	**Né'asètanôtse vé'keemahpe!**
Pass the butter!	**Né'asètanôtse heóveame**(or, **heóveamèške**)

Some words for different kinds of food are:

frybread **vétšéškévåhonoo'o**
berry pudding **menôtse** (Some people may call this
  énåhéno, the same as the word for gravy, following.)
gravy **énåhéno**
soup **hohpe**
potatoes **mésèhéstoto**
corn **måhaemenôtse** (This is kernel corn for
  eating.)
beans **monèškeho**
drymeat **honóvóhko**
bacon or salt pork **éškôseeséhotame** (The same word is used
  for pig, it literally means sharp- nosed-dog.)
cake **vé'keahonoo'o**
pie **tó'hovåhonoo'o**

Did you eat yet?	**Nééšemésèhehe?**
Héehe'e náéšeáahtse'mésèhéotse	Yes, I have eaten already.
No, I didn't eat yet.	**Násáa'éšemésèhéhe.**
I ate a lot.	**Náma'xemésehe.**
I ate a little.	**Nává'netšéške'mésehe.**

Commands:
  These are words for commands:

Come here!	**Nenáasèstse!**
Go on!	**Taanaasèstse!** (or, **Tanèšeamèhnèstse!**)
Come in!	**Estséhnèstse!** (or, **Né'éstséhnèstse!**,

  or **Esta'xèstse!**–the last word probably refers to more rapid
  movement.)
Don't do that! **Névé'nèhešéve!**

Sit down!	Hámèstoo'èstse! (a very common command)
Be quiet!	He'kotoo'èstse! (This can also refer to
sitting still.) Or, Ovánèhoo'èstse!	
Put it away!	Taénánôtse!
Let go of it!	Eneváénôtse! Or, Enánôtse!
Go to bed!	Tåhéovēšèstse!
Go to sleep!	Tanaóotsèstse!
Take your shoes off!	Né'tó'èstse!
Run!	Asèta'xèstse!
Wash your hands!	Nèše'šèhe'õnåtse!
Listen!	Aahtomónèstse! or, Aasèstsé'ôtse!
Listen to me!	Aahtovèstse!
Go buy bread!	Tåhéohtóvåtse kóhnôheo'o!
Go buy flour!	Tåhéohtóvåtse pénôhéó'o!
Get on!	Táxevonēhnèstse! (for example, 'Get on the
car, wagon, etc.!')	
Close the door!	Hoónôtse he'nétoo'o!
Open the door!	Onèstánôtse he'nétoo'o!
Read it!	Hoéstôtse!
Write it!	Môxe'oõhtse!
Wash the dishes!	Nèše'hānôtse hetóhkonôtse!
Sweep the floor!	Môxéhénèstse!
Take me to Lame Deer!	Néstse'oohé'tovèstse Méave'ho'ē no!
Naa máto ('or'), néssé'eohé'tovèstse!	
Tell it to him!	Mé'èstomeveha! Naa máto or tanèhešeha!
Say it!	Nèhešeha!
Say it again!	Hósenèhešeha! (or, Néxhósenèhešeha!)
Give me something to eat! Néxhoxomèstse! (Literally, 'Feed me!')	
Give me something to drink! Néxmanoxèstse!	
food	máhtáme, naa máto ('or'), mésèhestôtse
(Naa máto means 'also' or 'or'.)	
Let's go to town!	Nétåsé'eohtsema (måhoéve'ho'ēno)!
Let's go get our commodities! Nétanó'otsèstsénonèstse	
hoxotáhtotôtse!	
Let's go pick berries!	Nétåhéo'enemenama!

Let's go swimming!	**Nétåhétoo'hamema!** Or, **Nétåhéametó'honama!**
Let's go fishing!	**Nétåhénonónema!**
Tell me a story!	**Néxhóhta'heónaovêstse!**
Let's go play!	**Nétåhéevo'sóema!**
Come play with me!	**Néxhévêsto'sóemêstse!**
Let's go look on!	**Nétåhéve'hoosanema!** (This refers to being

a spectator at some function, especially a powwow, dance, or ball game.)

Let's go dance!	**Nétåhého'sóema!**
Let's go play handgame!	**Nétåhéno'oesenema!** (Many other

speakers say **Nétåhéno'oesanema!**)

Let's go ride horses!	**Nétåhétåhoenoneo'o mo'éhno'håme!**
Let's go rodeo!	**Nétåhévêsto'eétåhema!**
Turn the light on!	**Vó'ho'kåsénôtse!**
Turn the light out!	**Hó'továnôtse!**

Nouns:

In this next section we will practice saying some of the common nouns of Cheyenne. Every Cheyenne nouns belongs to a class of either Animate or Inanimate, or you might think of it as Living or Non-living. But sometimes there are words in the Living (Animate) category which we don't normally think of as being living. You'll see what we mean when you listen to the words.

In the Animate class are nouns referring to people, animals, spirits, and trees. Some "natural" objects are also considered animate, such as the sun, moon, star, and rock. Also some body parts are animate, and some articles of clothing, especially if they are made from cloth fibers. So here are some animate nouns:

Animate Nouns:

person	**vo'êstane**
woman	**hê'e**
man	**hetane**
child	**ka'êškóne**
dog	**oeškêso** (some people say **oeškese**)
cat	**póéso**

deer	váótséva
bird	vé'kése (some people say vé'késo)
God	Ma'hēõ'o
tree	hoohtsèstse
pine tree	šéstótó'e
sun	éše'he
moon	taa'e-éše'he (literally, 'night-sun')
star	hotohke
rock	ho'honáá'e
finger	mo'éško (homonym with inanimate mo'éško (ring)
coat	éstse'he (also can mean 'shirt')
blanket	hóoma
ball	hóhtséme

Inanimate Nouns:

car	amåho'hestõtse
house	måhēõ'o
arrow	maahe
liver	he'e
meat	ho'évohkõtse
pencil	mõxe'èstónestõtse (also can mean 'pen,' literally, 'writing-thing')
belt	hoestato
hat	hóhkèha'e

Singular and Plural Nouns:

Just like in English, Cheyenne nouns show whether they are singular or plural. By that we mean whether they refer to one thing or more than one thing. We will now give a few Cheyenne nouns. We will first give the singular and then we will give the plural.

MEANING	SINGULAR	PLURAL
baby	mé'èškevõtse	mé'èškevoto
bear	náhkohe	náhkõheo'o
bee	háhnoma	háhnomaho

14

cat	póeso	póesono
child	ka'èškóne	ka'èškóneho
dog	oeškẽso	oeškèseho
dress	hoestótse	hoestoto
duck	šé'še	šé'šeo'o
man	hetane	hetaneo'o
animal	hõva	hováhne
deer	váótséva	váotseváhne
beaver	hóma'e	homá'ne
	(also, homã'e 'beavers')	
goose	héna'e	hena'eo'o
	(also, henã'e 'geese')	
whiteman	vé'ho'e	vé'hó'e
horse	mo'éhno'ha	mo'éhno'hãme

Singular And Plural of Some Inanimate Nouns:

And now some inanimate nouns, again, first the singular and then the plural:

MEANING	SINGULAR	PLURAL
arrow	maahe	maahõtse
dish	hetohko	hetóhkonõtse
house	måhẽõ'o	måheonõtse
shoe	mo'keha	mo'kèhanõtse
bead	onéhávó'ke	onéhávó'èstse
hat	hóhkèha'e	hóhkèhá'èstse

Tape 1-B

Common Verbs:

In this next section we will practice saying some common verbs:

I'm eating	námésehe
Did you eat yet?	nééšemésèhehe?

I'm drinking **námane**
he's sleeping **énaóotse**
he's cooking **éhomõse** (Cheyenne does not differentiate between 'he' and 'she' in its pronominal prefix é-. This prefix simply indicates third person, so this verb could just as well be translated as 'she's cooking.')
he's slicing meat **éó'ĕsóva** (This verb is typically used for slicing meat when making drymeat.)
he is sewing **éhahpenó'e**
I'm writing **námŏxe'ĕstóne**
I'm going to school **námŏxe'ĕstóne** (refers to being a student, not the action of movement toward school; this is the same verb as 'I'm writing')
I'm reading **náhoéstóne** (also means 'I'm counting')
I'm praying **náháóéna**
I'm playing **náévo'soo'e**
I talk Cheyenne **nátsĕhésenestse**
Do you talk Cheyenne? **nétsĕhésenĕstsehe**
(Yes,) I talk Cheyenne a little **Tšéške'e nátsĕhésenestse, naa máto** ('or'), **nátšĕške'tsĕhésenestse.**
he's dancing **ého'soo'e**
he's working **éhotse'ohe**
he's teaching **évovéstomóséne** (many people say **évovéstomósáne**)
he's singing **énéméne**
they are singing **énémeneo'o**
he's afraid **ée'tóhtahe**
he's camping **évee'e**
he's happy **éhetótaetãno, naa máto, épåhávetãno** (or, **épĕhévetãno**)
it's big **éma'haõ'o, naa máto, étåhpe'o**
Is it big? **éma'hao'ohe? naa máto, étåhpe'ohe?**
épĕhéva'e it's good
its hard (difficult) **éhótoanáto**
éhe'anáto it's easy
éonénĕšeotse it's broke down (or, broken)

it's boiling	**éhéesevo'ta**
it is burning	**ééxo'ãse**
étónetoeme	How much is it? (or, What's the price?)
it's high priced	**éháaoeme**
it's inexpensive	**éhe'anávoeme** (literally, 'it's easy-priced')
Do you like it?	**Népêhévatsêstahe?**
I like it	**Nápåhávátsésta** (or, **Nápêhévátsésta**).
I want it	**náho'ahe**

I want them (inanimate things)   **náho'åhenôtse**

I want berries   **Náho'åhenôtse menôtse, naa máto** (or), **menôtse náho'åhenôtse.** (This example shows that, in some way, word order is flexible within Cheyenne sentences.)

I want a horse   **Náho'åhenôtse mo'éhno'ha,**
or, **mo'éhno'ha náho'åhenôtse.**

(Although the last two verbs are identical in spelling, they are actually grammatically different: 'berries' are inanimate and plural, and the verb with it is inflected for this inanimacy and plurality, whereas 'horse' is animate and singular and the verb with it is inflected for this animacy and singularity. The verbs will have different spellings of their suffixes when the object of the verb is animate and plural, as in the next example.)

I want cats   **Náho'åhénoto póesono.**
I'm tired   **Nákåhaneotse.** (Notice that the **k** in the Cheyenne word has a hard, or aspirated, sound.)
I'm not tired yet   **Násáa'éšekåhaneotséhe.**
Are you tired?   **Nééšekåhaneotsehe, naa máto,**
nékåhaneotsehe? (The first verb listed here literally means, 'Are you tired yet?' Notice that the question form of a verb ends with the suffix **-he** but the vowel before it is low-pitched. But in the preceding negative verb, **násáa'éšekåhaneotséhe**, there is also a suffix **-he**, but it behaves differently, causing the vowel before it to be high-pitched. Technically (or, to use linguistic terminology, phonemically), the two suffixes are actually different.)

Practice with the Verb 'to see':

I see him	návóómo
I saw bears	návóomoo'o náhkôheo'o
I see you	névóomåtse ('I saw you' is the

same, névóomåtse.)

Do you see me?   névóomehe?

he saw me   návóoma

we (exclusive)   návóomóne (This Cheyenne 'we'
excludes the person, or persons, the speaker is talking to.)

I saw it   návóóhta

I saw cars   Návóohtanôtse amåho'héstotôtse.

Did you see cars?   Névóohtanotse amåho'héstotôtse?
(Notice that the difference between this question and the
preceding statement is that the question verb has a voiced vowel on
its next-to-the-last (penultimate) vowel, while in the statement verb
that vowel is voiceless.)

I didn't see him	násáavóomóhe
I didn't see the bears	násáavóomóheo'o náhkôheo'o
I didn't see it	násáavóóhtóhe
I didn't see the cars	násáavóohtôhenôtse amåho' héstotôtse
I'm looking at him	návé'hóómo
I'm looking at the children	návé'hoomoo'o ka'êškóneho
Look at him!	Vé'hoomeha!
Look at the children!	Vé'hoomenáno ka'êškóneho!
Look at the cars!	Vé'hóóhtôtse amåho'héstotôtse!

I know it	náhéne'ēna
Do you know it?	Néhéne'enahe?

(In case you should wonder, there is really no significance in
this booklet as to whether or not a Cheyenne word which itself
translates as (or begins a phrase which translates as) a complete
sentence in English starts with a capital letter or not. 'Do you know
(understand) it (now)?' Nétaéšêhéne'enahe? (Another English
translation of the Cheyenne would be 'Do you understand it yet?'

18

The Cheyenne word for 'now,' **hétsetseha** does not occur in this verb on the tape, although it could if we were actually focusing upon the time of NOW, which we are not doing here.)

I understand it (now)	**nátaéšêhéne'ēna**
I love him	**náméhóto**
I caught him	**nánåha'ēno**
I'm chasing him	**nánéhóvo**
I found him	**námé'óvo**
I hit him	**náoõmo**
I depend on him	**náne'étamenôtse**

Different Kinds of People:

Now we will have some words for different kinds of people:

baby	**mé'êškevôtse, naa máto** ('or'), **mé'êševôtse**
child	**ka'êškóne**
young man	**kåsováåhe**
young woman	**kåse'ééhe**
man	**hetane**
woman	**hẽ'e**
old man	**ma'háhkéso**
old lady	**måhtamåhááhe**
teacher	**vovéstomósenéhe** (many people say **vovéstomósanéhe**)
policeman	**matanaéve'ho'e**
doctor	**naa'éve'ho'e**
pharmacist	**heséeotséve'ho'e**
lawyer	**ho'emanéhe** (also means 'judge')
cook	**homôséve'ho'e**
(B.I.A.) superintendent	**méavé'ho'e**
council member	**me'ko**
mé'kono	tribal council
preacher	**ma'heóneéestséhetane** (literally, holy speaking man)

butcher	na'tónetane
nurse	naa'éve'ho'á'e
cowboy	tóhé'kèsaéve'ho'e
secretary	móxe'èstónéhe
watchman	tséne'evávóósénèstse (many people say
	tséne'evávóósánèstse; the word can also refer to
	'umpire' or 'guard')

Relatives (Kinship Terms):

Our next section will be about words for relatives:

Do you have children?	Néhenésonêhehe?
Yes, I have children	Héehe'e náhenésone.
He is my son	Náhee'hahenótse.
She is my daughter	Náhestónåhenótse.
She is my mother	Náheškenótse.
He is my father	Náhéhenótse.
How are you related to him?	Nétónetoémo?
He/she is my brother/sister/cousin	Náhevésêsónenótse.
He is my grandfather	Náhemêšémenótse.
She is my grandmother	Náhevéškemenótse
They are my relatives	Náhevóohestovenoto
He is my friend	Náhevésenéhenótse (Used
only by a man about a man friend.)	

Naa hê'e, náhevése'enótse   And a woman (says), 'she is
my friend.' (Used only by a woman about a woman friend.)

my father	ného'éehe
my mother	náhko'éehe
my grandfather	namêšéme
my grandmother	néške'éehe
my son	nae'ha
my daughter	nåhtona

How To Address Your Relative:

Next are a few words for relatives, the way that you speak to
them. Linguists often call these words vocatives. These are the

words that you use to address your relative:

father	**ného'e**
mother	**náhko'e**
grandmother	**néške'e**
grandfather	**námèšeme** (Notice that this is the same as

'my grandfather,' given in the preceding section, except that the
high pitch on the word is now on the first vowel.)
friend, or brother **hóovéhe**

Your Relative:

Now a few words for your relative:

your father	**eho**
your mother	**neško**
your grandmother	**éškeme**
your grandfather	**nemèšéme**
your grandchild	**éxahe**

Questions and Answers:

This next section has some more questions and answers:

What's your name?	**Nétónèševéhe?**
Aénohe Oxháa'ého'oese náheševéhe	My name is High Hawk
Kovááhe náheševéhe	My name is Youngman.
Náhkòhéso náheševéhe	My name is Youngbear.
Påháveameõhtse náheševéhe	My name is Walks Nice.
Vóestaa'e náheševéhe	My name is White Buffalo Woman.
Hotóhké'e náheševéhe	My name is Star Woman.
Nétsèhésevéhehe?	Do you have a Cheyenne name?
What are you doing?	**Nétónèšéve?**
I'm working	**náhotse'ohe**
I'm not doing anything	**násáatónèšévéhe**
Where do you live?	**Tósa'e néhoo'e?** (Another way to

say 'Where do you live?' (is), **Tósa'e névo'èstanéheve?**)
Mo'òhtávòheomenéno návo'èstanéheve I live in Lame Deer.
Vóhpoométanéno návo'èstanéheve I live in Busby.
Naa máto (And also), **Oévemanåhéno náhoo'e** I live in Birney.

Totoemanåhéno návo'êstanéheve   I live in Ashland
Onónéno náhoo'e   I live in the Ree district (between Busby and
   Muddy Creek district)
Héne 'tósa'e névo'êstanéheve,' tséxhenove, heva máto
   'tósa'e néhoo'e,' éme'henove, When you say, 'Where do you
live?' or 'Where do you stay?' you would say it that way. (During
checking of these materials, Mr. Risingsun said he would now
prefer to use the Cheyenne word **naa** 'and,' instead of **heva**
'maybe,' in this sentence.)

Where did you go?	**Tósa'e ného'õhtse?**
I went to Lame Deer	**Méave'ho'ēno nátåho'õhtse.**
I went to Ashland	**Totoemanåhéno nátåho'õhtse.**
I went to Kingfisher	**Noma'hé-o'hé'e nátåho'õhtse.**
I went to Oklahoma City	**Ma'xepóno'e nátåho'õhtse.**
Where are you going (now)?	**Tósa'e néamêho'õhtse?**
I am going to Billings	**E'êxováhtóva námêho'õhtse.**
I'm going to Hardin	**He'konemåhoéve'ho'ēno**
	náamêho'õhtse.
I'm going to Watonga	**Tséhma'êho'a'ē'ta nátsêhe'õhtse.**

   (The last word is another way of saying that you are going to a
   certain place.)

Where did you come from?	**Tósa'e nénêxhé'óhtse?**
I came from Busby	**Vóhpoométanéno nánêxhé'óhtse.**
I came from Colstrip	**Ho'óseo'hé'e nánêxhé'óhtse.**
Where do you work?	**Tósa'e néhotse'ohe?**
I work in Lame Deer	**Méave'ho'ēno náhotse'ohe.**
I work at the Big Store	**Ma'xêhohtóvamåheóne**
	náhotse'ohe.
I work at the BIA building	**Méamåheóne náhotse'ohe.**
I work at the school	**Môxe'êstónemåheóne náhotse'ohe.**

What are you going to do tomorrow?   **Néto'seméotónêšéve?** (The
   "preverb" **méo-** within the verb refers to 'morning;' in this
   case, the meaning of 'tomorrow morning' is generalized to
   'tomorrow.')
I'm going shopping in Billings
   Náto'sêtsêhešêhéohtóva E'êxováhtóva.

I'm going to see the doctor
Nátao'sêhévé'hóómo naa'éve'ho'e.

I'm going to a basketball game in Colstrip
Nátao'sêhéve'hoomoo'o éto'seevo'sóeo'o Ho'óseo'hé'e.
(Literally, 'I'm going to watch them; they are going to play in Colstrip.')

I'm going to the Crow Fair   **Nátao'sêtsêhe'õhtse Ooetanéno tsé'amo'eétåhénove.**

I'm going to preach in Hammon   **Náto'sêtšêhešeéestse Eše'hôhma'åhevẽno.**

I'm going to be slicing up meat   **Náto'seó'êsóva.**

When are you leaving?   **Tóse'še néto'seaseohe?**

I'm going to leave tomorrow   **Måhvóonão'o nátao'seaseohe.**

I'm going to leave next week
Nátao'seaseohema'tåhóseamêstôheéno'e.

I'm going to leave this evening   **Hetóéva nátao'seaseohe.**

I'm going to leave on Monday
No'ka ma'éšeeve nátao'seaseohe.
(Note: In Oklahoma the word for 'Monday' here would be **Ma'énema'heóneéšeeve**, literally, 'when it will be the end of the holy- day' here, instead of **No'ka ma'éšeeve**, meaning, literally, 'when it will be the first day.')

When did you come back home?
Tóne'še néévåho'êhóó'óhtse?

I came back yesterday   **Ešeẽva náévåho'êhóó'óhtse.**

We came back on Tuesday
Náévåho'êhóo'ôhtséme nexa tsé'éšeeve.
(Note: In Oklahoma substitute **No'ka tsé'éšeeve** for **Nexa tsé'éšeeve** (literally, 'the second day') here.)

I got back this morning   **Tséhvóonā'o náévåho'eohe.**

Where are your children?   **Naa nenésoneho?**

They're in school   **Naaémôxe'êstóneo'o (or,étåhéhoéstoneo'o).**

They're sliding down (for example, sledding) **Etåhéanåha'xeo'o.**

They're skating   **Etåhésevanoo'o.**

Where is your father?   **Naa eho?**

He's working   **Etåhéhotse'ohe, naa máto, éhotse'ohe.**

He's sleeping	Enaóotse.
He went drinking	Etåhémaneõhtse.
I don't know where he is	Násáahéne'enóhe tséståho'õhtsèse,
naa máto, násáahéne'enovóhe tséståho'õhtse.	
What is this?	Hénová'éto hé'tóhe?
It's a pencil	Naa môxe'èstónestôtse.
It is a choker	Naa ho'ota.
It is a necklace	Naa ho'ota. (The word ho'ota
	means either 'choker' or 'necklace.')
It is a drumstick (for drumming)	(Naa) pó'ponôheónó'è.
It is a war bonnet	(Naa) mámaa'e.
It's a bustle	(Naa) hóxe'èséneo'o.
What is that?	Hénová'e há'tóhe?
It's a fence	(Naa) éamóneane.
It's a binder, or bailer	(Naa) hohpo'oéseo'o.
It's a threshing machine, or combine	(Naa) óenenestôtse.
Who is this?	Névááéso tsé'tóhe?
It's a bullsnake	(Naa) ne'e'e.
He's my grandson	Náhevéxahenôtse.
It's a beetle	(Naa) háméško.
Who is that man?	Névááéso tá'tóhe hetane?
Oh, that's Joe.	Naa Ho'évåhtamẽhnèstse. (The
Indian name here means 'Earth Walking,' or, more precisely,	
'Walking on the Earth.')	

That's my son	nae'ha.
That's the BIA Superintendant	méavé'ho'e.
Who's that old lady?	Névááéso tá'tóhe måhtamåhááhe?
That's my grandma.	néške'éehe.
That's Maude	Ma'séeota'e. (The name means 'Red
(Herbal) Medicine Woman.')	
What time is it?	Tóne'še ého'oésta?
It's noon	Esétovoésta.
It's 3 o'clock	Ena'nôxe'ohe.
It's 5 o'clock	Enóhonôxe'ohe.

Is it time to go to bed? **Eéšêho'oéstahe tséohkêhe'še-**
ovêšenáhtove?

Yes   **Héehe'e.**

How much does this cost? **Etónetoeme?**

Ten dollars   **Emåhtóhtôhnoeme.**

$1.50   **Na'êstse naa o'xe.**

It's $30   **Ena'nó'oeme.**

What's your telephone number?

                      Etónetôxe'ohe neaseéestsestôtse?

It's 984-1737   **sóohto na'nohto neve na'êstse nésohto**
na'he nésohto.

Which is your house? **Táase nemåhêõ'o?**

It's the white one   **Há'tóhe tsévó'ómo.**

Which is your car?   **Táase neamåho'hestôtse?**

It's the blue one   **Há'tóhe tséotá'távo.**

Which dog is yours?   **Táasévoo'o oeškêso nêstôtse?**
    (Literally, 'Which dog is your pet?')

It's the black one   **Tá'tóhe tsémo'kôhtávóvåtse.**

Tape 2-A

Questions and Answers (continued):

Is that your roan horse? Tá'tóhe ma'ováhe nêstotséhahe?
Yes, I own him Héehe'e náá'éno.
Did you sell your red pickup?Néhohtóvahe nema'eamévôhtó'-
hestôtse? (Many speakers pronounce the second word as
nema'eamóvôhtó'hestôtse.)
Yes, it just got worn out Héehe'e, étó'tšêšetaomemâhoveotse.

Talking About Cheyenne:

In this next section we will have some words and questions and
phrases to help people who are trying to learn Cheyenne, words
about learning Cheyenne.

Do you talk Cheyenne? Nétsêhésenêstsehe?
Yes, I talk Cheyenne Héehe' nátsêhésenestse.
I talk Cheyenne a little bit Nátšêške'tsêhésenestse.
I can understand but do not speak it well. Náohkenanéáhta
  naa oha násáapêhévetsêhésenêstséhe.
I want to speak Cheyenne Nátsêhésenêstsétáno.
I want to learn Cheyenne
  Náhéne'enátanó'ta Tsêhésenêstsestôtse.
Speak Cheyenne to me! Néstsêhésenêstovêstse!
What is Hardin called in Cheyenne?
  Etónêšêtsêhéseóxôhestohe 'Hardin'?
Naa He'konemâhoéve'ho'êno Well, it's called 'Hard-town.'
How is it said, 'He is smiling'? Etónêšetsêhésto'-
anéstove 'He is smiling'?
(Note: The various verbs used in this section for asking how to
say something are similar in meaning. The verb in this particular
question means, literally, 'How is it pronounced in Cheyenne?')
Naa éxaéméné'o. Well, 'he's smiling.'

How do you say, 'He is drunk'?,
Etónêšêtsêhéseóxôhenove 'He is drunk'?
Naa énonótovåše'še. Well, he is drunk.

(The question asked here means, literally, 'How is it said in Cheyenne?' The Impersonal suffixes -stove (phonemically, /-htove/) and -nove appear to have no difference in meaning. Some speakers seem to use -htove almost exclusively, while others, like Mr. Risingsun, speaking on the tape, use both suffixes, as can be seen by comparing the suffix of the question verb here with that of the preceding question. The linguistic category Impersonal means that a verb has no specific subject referent, rather, the action of the verb is viewed as being done by people in general, that is, people that the speaker refers to in a generic way. Some reasonable English translations of Cheyenne Impersonal verbs could contain a generic 'you' (as in the English question asked here, 'How do you say, ...?'), 'it' (as we have noted in the literal meaning of the Cheyenne question here), or 'they' (we could have translated the Cheyenne question here as, 'How do they say, ...?'). Or, an English translation of an Impersonal verb could begin with the phrase 'There is ...,' hence, **ého'sóestove** can be translated as 'they are dancing,' or, 'there is dancing going on;' it contrasts with **ého'sóeo'o** 'they are dancing,' where the speaker is referring to a specific group of people.)

How would you say, 'Pray for me!'?
Etónêšêtsêhésto'anéstove 'Pray for me!'?
Naa néxháoenavomotaxêstse. ('Well, pray for me.')
Did I say it right?　　　**Nápêhévo'anehe?**
Yes, you said it right.　　**Héehe'e, népêhévó'áne.**
You almost said it right; try again!
　　Nééšêto'sêpåhávó'áne; vóvôhetó'ánêstse! (The first verb, as
　　usual, can also be pronounced, **Nééšêto'sêpêhévó'áne.**)
What did you say?　　　**Néóxôheve?**
What did he say?　　　　**Eóxôhevoo'o?**
I didn't say anything　　**Násáa'óxôhéhe.**
Say it again!　　　　　　**Hósenêhešeha!**
Say it louder!　　　　　　**Tåhpe'eéestsêstse!**

Påháveááhtôtse tsétó'taehénove!	Listen to exactly the way it is said!
Is that it?	**Hénêsehe?**

(This might be asked about some word the speaker was searching for.)

Héehe'e, hena'háanéhe	Yes, that's it.
What does that mean?	**Hénová'e tsénêhestohe?**
Can a woman say that?	**Hẽ'e éme'vésenêhehe?**
Héehe'e, hẽ'e éme'vésenêhevoo'o	Yes, a woman can say that.

No, a woman can't say that
Hová'åháne, hẽ'e éme'sáavésenêhéhe.
Do young people understand that word?
Tsémóneéšeestse éhéne'enahe héne éestsestôtse?
Is there a better way of saying it?   **Epåhávêhóxe'enêstsé'tôhehe?**

Obviation:

In the Cheyenne language when there are two people, and you're talking about them, and one person is doing something to the other person, the grammar changes in a special way. The technical word for this is called 'obviation.' It happens in all Algonquian languages, like Cheyenne. Listen carefully and we'll show you some of the examples, and you can practice on your own, and practice with someone else.

First we'll say some common nouns in the regular (proximate) way they are said, and then listen as the ending of the nouns changes a little bit when we use them for when one person does something to another person. Also, the ending on the verbs changes a little bit. Because of this, along with the common nouns, we will also give a few common verbs in which the grammar will be 'I am doing SOMETHING to him.' So, you can listen to the change between 'I am doing SOMETHING to him,' and 'he is doing SOMETHING to SOMEONE ELSE.'

man	**hetane**
woman	**hẽ'e**
child	**ka'êškóne**

duck	šé'še
deer (singular)	váótséva
fish (singular)	nóma'he
young man	kåsovááhe
her mother	heške
her husband	heéháme
a Crow person	Ooetane

I saw him	návóómo
I ate him	námévo
I love him	náméhóto
I fought him	náméóto

I saw the man	Návóómo hetane.
I saw a duck	Návóómo šé'še.
I love that young man	Náméhóto néhe kåsovááhe.
Náméóto néhe Ooetane	I fought that Crow.

He saw a man	Evóomóho hetanóho.
He saw a woman	Evóomóho he'óho.
He saw a child	Evóomóho ka'êškóneho.
He saw a duck	Evóomóho še'xo.
She loved that young man	Eméhoto néhe kåsováaheho.
She loves her mother	Eméhoto heške.
He fought that Crow	Eméoto néhe Ooetanóho.

I ate a duck	Námévo šé'še.
He ate a duck	Emevo še'xo.

Her mother loves her	Eméhótáá'e heške. (That is, 'She is loved by her (own) mother.')
Her husband loves her	Heéháme éméhótáá'e.
A Crow fought against him	Eméótáá'e Ooetanóho.
He was seen by that man	Evóomáá'e néhe hetanóho.

Independent and Conjunct Order Verbs:

In English grammar teachers often talk about Independent and Dependent, or Subordinate, clauses. The Cheyenne language, along with other Algonquian languages, has a similar type of division among the verbs. The regular verbs, or the most common way of saying them, we say are in the Independent Order. And the dependent verbs, or you might say a kind of subordinate verbs, we say are of the Conjunct Order. The terms Independent and Conjunct are used by linguists who work with Algonquian languages.

We will now have some practice with verbs from these two classes of orders. We will give verbs in their Independent Order and we will also have verbs in the Conjunct Order. Listen carefully to the differences that take place in the verbs.

First, some verbs of the Independent Order:

I saw him	návóómo
I'm married to him	návéstoẽmo
I hit him	náoõmo
he's sleeping	énaóotse
he made it	émanẽstse
I helped him	návéståhémo
he helped me	návéståhema
they helped me	návéståhémáá'e
I ate it	námese
I saw it	návóóhta
I want it	náho'ahe
I have it	náhó'tse

Conjunct Verbs with Questions:

Now the verbs will be in the Conjunct Order. This can often occur in questions, but it can also occur in regular sentences, also. First we will have them with some questions. We will be making 'Who?' and 'What?' questions. Listen to those question words, first, by themselves. (Cheyenne verbs in such questions are said to be Conjunct Participles. A Conjunct Participle is something like a relative clause in English.)

Who?	Néváahe?
Who (plural)?	Neváeseo'o?
Another way of saying Who? (is)	Néváéso?
Who (obviative)?	Neváesóho?

What?	Hénová'e? (or,) Hénáá'e?
What things (plural)?	Hénová'ehôtse?

Who do you see?	Néváahe tsévóomôtse?
Who saw you?	Néváahe tsévóomáta'e?
Who is he married to?	Neváesóho tsévéstoemose?
Who hit me?	Néváahe tséoomã'êstse?
Who is that sleeping?	Néváéso néhe tsénaóotsêstse?

He is singing (Independent Order)	Enéméne.
He's praying (Independent Order)	Eháóéna.
He's eating (Independent Order)	Emésehe.

Who is that singing?	Néváéso tá'tóhe tsénéménêstse?
Who prayed?	Néváéso tséháóénåtse?
Who ate?	Néváahe tséméseestse?
Who (plural) hit you?	Neváeseo'o tséoomata'óse?
Who (plural) did you see?	Neváeseo'o tsévóomóse?
Who did you help?	Néváahe tsévéståhemôtse?
Who helped him?	Neváesóho tsévéståhémaese?

What are you eating?	Hénová'e tséméseto?
What do you see?	Hénáá'e tsévóohtomo?
What do you want?	Hénáá'e tsého'åheto?
What are you making?	Hénová'e tsémanêstseto?
What is he making?	Hénová'etse tsémanêstsêse?

(Note that the Cheyenne 'What?' question word here has a different ending from the 'What?' word in the preceding question.

The Cheyenne question word here is an obviative. At this point you might want to refer back to the previous introductory remarks about Cheyenne obviation, or to pages in the Cheyenne reference grammar (such as pages 20-21 and 171) which discuss obviation. Although grammatically obviated inanimate nouns are pronounced exactly the same as proximate inanimate nouns, question words and verbs associated with obviated inanimate entities DO take obviative suffixes, as we have seen here with this 'What?' question word. The 'in-focus' (proximate) entity in this question is the person who is making something. Since only one third person may be proximate at any one time, the thing which this (proximate) person is making is referred to by **Hénová'etse** 'What?,' which has an obviative suffix. We will return to this matter of obviation, again, in the next section when we present some possessed nouns.)

What does he want?	**Hénová'etse tsého'aese?**
What did he see?	**Hénová'etse tsévóóhto?**
What do you have?	**Hénová'e tsého'tseto?**
What (plural) do you have?	**Hénová'ehôtse tsého'tseto?**

(Note that the English here sounds awkward. This is necessary to try to reflect the fact that Cheyenne marks a difference in question words depending on whether or not the things or people they refer to are singular or plural. We could make the English question sound more natural by saying something like 'What things do you have?')

What (plural) do you want?	**Hénová'ehôtse tsého'åheto?**

More Conjunct Order Verbs:

Now we will have a few sentences with verbs of the Conjunct Order but without question words in the sentences:

I love my spouse	**Náméhóto tsévéstoemo.**
I saw him when he was praying	**Návóómo tséxháóénåse.**

(Note that the conjunct verb here is spelled slightly differently from the conjunct verb in the last section, **tséháóénåtse**, that was in the question which translated to English as 'Who prayed?' The earlier verb is a Conjunct Participle. Conjunct Participles with third person subjects have a /t/ in their ending. The corresponding Conjunct verb here, tséxháóénâse, lacks a /t/. We shall call this latter kind of verb a Conjunct Order Adverbial.)

I saw you when you were eating Névóomâtse tséhmésêheto.
(The second verb here is also a Conjunct Order Adverbial. Notice that past tense is marked by /h/ immediately following the tsé- Conjunct prefix. The x of the preceding Conjunct verb, tséxháóénâse 'when he was praying' is one of the ways that this /h/ past tense marker is pronounced.)

I saw the man who was singing Návóómo hexane tsénéménêstse.
(Note that this Conjunct verb has a /t/ in its ending, showing that it is a Conjunct Participle. Notice, also, how this Conjunct verb translates as a relative clause in English. We noted this fact about Conjunct Participles in a parenthesized (not occurring on the tape) introductory remark to this entire section on Conjunct verbs.)

He saw the one who was singing Tsénémenétsese évóomóho.
(The Conjunct verb here, the first word, is obviated.)

It's morning Eéševóonâ'o. (That was in the Independent Order.)
I sang this morning Náméonéméne, also, Nánéméne tséhvóonâ'o.
(The second way of translating the English sentence here has a Conjunct Order Adverbial verb, 'when it was morning.')
He sang this morning Tséhvóona'otse énéméne.
(The Conjunct verb here, the first word, is obviated because the 'he' of the verb 'to sing' is 'in focus,' or proximate.)
I was sleeping when you ate Nánaóotse tséhmésêheto

Conjunct Verbs with Other Prefixes:

As you have heard, many Conjunct Order verbs begin with the prefix tsé-. However, there are other Conjunct prefixes, and here are a few sentences with some other Conjunct prefixes. Listen carefully:

Whenever it snows I just stay home
> Oxho'éetoo'èstse navénóvo náohkèhe'kotoo'e.

If it's sunny tomorrow we'll go for a picnic
> Måhvé'méopèhévatamáno'e nèstao'hémèsèhema.

I don't know whether it rained
> Násáahéne'enóhe éóhoo'kõho.

Even if I am poor I will depend on God
> Hó'nèšèháo'omenèhéto nåhtsene'étamenòtse Ma'hēõ'o.

Even if the weather is bad tomorrow we will go to Billings
> Hó'nèšeméohoháatamáno'e nèstaváhtometsèhe'òhtsema
> E'èxováhtóva.

I wish all the children spoke Cheyenne
> Momóxemåhetsèhésenèstsévòtse ka'èškóneho.

I guess he must have not felt well
> Móho'nópèhevomóhtaestse.

When the Savior returns how shall we answer him?
> Naa máhne'évåho'ēhnèstseVo'èstanévèstómanéhe
> nèstónèšeno'èstovone?

Next summer we will go to the powwow in Lame Deer
> Ma'tåhóseméaneve nèståhéve'hoosenémáne Méave'ho'ēno.
> (The second verb is pronounced nèståhéve'hoosanémáne by
> many speakers.)

Possessed Nouns:

In this next section we will practice saying possessive nouns,
such as 'my car,' 'your house,' 'your shoes,' and so forth.

Inanimate Possessed Nouns:

my house	namåhēõ'o
your house	nemåhēõ'o
his house	hemåhēõ'o
our (exclusive) house	namåheónáne
our (inclusive) house	nemåheónane

(Notice that there were two ways of saying 'our house;' this is
a very important part of Cheyenne grammar. The first way, starting

34

with the prefix **na-**, means 'our' which does NOT include the person you are speaking to. The second way of saying 'our' INCLUDES the person you are speaking to and begins with the prefix **ne-**. In technical language, when you are just speaking without including the person you are speaking to, it is called "exclusive 'we'." And when you include the person you are speaking to, it is called "inclusive 'we'."

your (pl.) house	**nemåheónévo**
their house	**hemåheónévo**
my cap	**navóhkêha'e**
	(Note that unpossessed 'cap' is **hóhkêha'e**.)
my caps	**navóhkêhá'êstse**
their caps	**hevóhkêha'evótse**

Animate Possessed Nouns:

The possessed nouns we have practiced so far have been inanimate. Next we will practice saying some possessed nouns which are animate. Listen carefully when we talk about something being possessed by a third person, that is, how we would translate in English 'his,' or 'her,' or 'their ___.' Earlier in these language learning lessons we talked about something called obviation in Cheyenne. Obviation also occurs with animate nouns whenever they are possessed by a third person. It may sound complicated at first, but if you listen carefully, you'll see how the endings of the nouns change to indicate this obviation when the prefixes change from **na-**, that is, first person, or **ne-**, second person, to **he-**, third person.

my pet	**nåhtõtse**
your pet	**nêstõtse**
his pet	**hestotseho**
their pets	**hestotséhevóho**
my daughter	**nåhtona**
my daughters	**nåhtónaho**

his daughters	hestónaho

(Can also mean 'his daughter,' that is, in Cheyenne an obviated noun may be translated as either singular or plural.)

their daughter(s)	hestónåhevóho

my son	nae'ha
our (exclusive) son	nae'hahãne
his son(s)	hee'haho

Some Different Possessive Prefixes:

When you are talking about some of your relatives, for a few of the words the possessive prefixes are slightly different. Instead of **na-** for first person, you will hear a high-pitched **né** for first person, and a high-pitched **é** for second person. So, listen to a few of these examples and practice them:

my friend	néséne

(only a man can say this about a man friend)

your friend	éséne
his friend	hevésenóho
my grandmother	néške'éehe
your grandmother	éškeme
his grandmother	hevéškemo
my father	ného'éehe
your father	eho
his father	heho
our (inclusive) father	éhane
their father(s)	héhevóho

Verb Obviation With Possessed Nouns:

Even though obviation does not occur on possessed inanimate nouns, verbs which are associated with those possessed inanimate nouns do reflect obviation. And the same thing occurs with animate nouns: As we've said before, when animate nouns are possessed by a third person, they become obviated, and also verbs associated with these obviated animate possessed nouns are also obviated.

Listen to some examples:

My house is red	Namåhēō'o émá'o.
His house is red	Hemåhēō'o éma'otse.
My car is yellow	Naamåho'hestôtse éheóvo.

Tape 2-B

Verb Obviation With Possessed Nouns (continued):

His car is yellow	Heamåho'hestôtse éheóvotse.
My son is sick	Nae'ha éháomóhtahe.
His son is sick	Hee'haho éháomóhtåhóho.

My friend is good-natured
 Néséne épåhávoéstomo'he (or, épêhévoéstomo'he).
His friend is good-natured
 Hevésenóho épåhávoéstomo'ho (or, épêhévoéstomo'ho).

My daughter sang	Nåhtona énéméne.
His daughter(s) sang	Hestónaho énémenóho.

Numbers:

The next section is about Cheyenne numbers:

Do you know numbers?	Nééšêhéne'enanotse hoéstonêstotôtse?
Yes, I know some of them	Héehe'e, hosêstse náhéne'enanôtse.
Say them to me!	Néhnêhéstôtse!

First, numbers for counting things: éestséstotôtse
 ôxhoemee'êstse hová'ehôtse, (words for counting things):

one person	na'êstse vo'êstane
two cats	neše póesono
three houses	na'he måheónôtse

four children	neve ka'ěškóneho
five belts	noho hoestátónėstse
six men	naesohto hetaneo'o
seven women	nésohto he'eo'o
eight dogs	na'nohto oeškėseho
nine trees	sóohto hoóhtseto
ten sticks	måhtohto kåhamãxėstse

Now, numbers for how many times something occurred: tónėstoha tséstónėšévenove, (how many times it was done):

once	no'ka
twice	nexa
thrice	na'ha
four times	neva
five times	nóhona
six times	naesóhtoha
seven times	nésôhtoha
eight times	na'nóhtoha
nine times	sóohtoha
ten times	måhtóhtoha

For example, I went to Oklahoma twice   Hámó'ôhtse, nátatsėhe'õhtse Heévåhetanéno nexa.

This ends the basic lessons in this Cheyenne language learning course. You have been exposed to the basic grammar, although some of the time we have not presented it in a formal way. If you wish further information about some of the grammatical things that we have touched upon, we recommend that you study one or more of the books that have been published about the Cheyenne language. Check with a college library near you, and you should be able to find a copy of a Cheyenne dictionary, or maybe there will be several dictionaries. There are copies of Cheyenne language materials at the Dull Knife Memorial College (John Woodenlegs Memorial Library) in Lame Deer, Montana, and there are Cheyenne materials at Southwestern Oklahoma (University) in Weatherford, Oklahoma, and also at the University of Oklahoma in Norman. See page 57 of this booklet, also, for further information about materials that you can consult for more formal study.

Sample Conversations:

From here on in the tape we will present practice conversations. We will only give English to set the background for each conversation. And then, from now on we will just use Cheyenne in the actual conversations. You may consult your booklet to see the translation of the Cheyenne material.

Going Berry-Picking:

(This is one of several conversations on this tape (the others are "Imogene Visits Josephine," "You Talk Cheyenne, Too?" and "Helping at the Birney Powwow") which Mrs. Glenmore helped Mr. Leman design, before her death. These conversations appear in the book, **Náévåhóo'ôhtséme/We Are Going Back Home: Cheyenne History and Stories Told by James Shoulderblade and Others,** edited by Wayne Leman, 1987.

The book has been available for $48.00 from:

Voices of Rupert's Land Fund
c/o John D. Nichols
Department of Native Studies
532 Fletcher Argue Building
University of Manitoba
Winnipeg, MAN. R3T 2N2
CANADA

The conversations appear here by permission of Mr. Leman. Occasionally the taped version is slightly different from the printed version that appears in the book.)

The first conversation is about going berry- picking. A lady named Imogene (Mr. Risingsun's wife) arrives at her friend's house. Her friend is named Josephine (Glenmore), in English. Josephine's name in Cheyenne is **Voestaa'e**, which means 'White Buffalo Woman.'

Imogene=I
Josephine=J

I: **Vóestaa'e, néhoehe?** Josephine, are you home?
J: **Náhoo'e, éstséhnèstse!** I'm home, come in!
I: **Mónèståhósèhéo'enemenámáne?** Shall we (inclusive) go berry-picking again?
J: **Naa nèståhénòhtsevóohtánonèstse Kovááhe tsénèhestose.** Well, we'll go look for the ones (berries) that Youngman (Mr. Leman) told about.
I: **Nómòheto!** Let's go!
J: **Naa Má'háéso éto'sevé'háhtse.** Old Man (Josephine's affectionate nickname for her husband) is gonna go along.
I: **Héehe'e tsetakánomeasetåxe'ovóho náhkòhóho.** Yes, he'll scare bear(s) away. (This is humorous, especially since a bear would seldom be seen, and given the social relations of the participants.)
J: **Nêstanovo'émáne. Nåháóhe nèståhetóevemésèhémáne. Náhe'óhtánóne honóvóhko naa éškòseeséhotame naa mésèhéstoto.** We'll (inclusive) take a lunch along. Over there we'll eat (supper). We (exclusive) have leftover drymeat and salt pork and potatoes.
I: **Etootõmo hétsetseha. Esáaheómèsèhoháaeho'táhane.** It's cool now. It's not as hot as it's been.
J: **Nóheto!** Let's go!

Shopping at the Arts and Crafts Store:
In our next conversation a man named John stops by the Arts and Crafts Center in Lame Deer.

John=J
Carol Whitewolf (store manager)=C

J: **Påhávevóonã'o.** Good morning.

C: **Héehe'e, épêhévatamáno'e.** Yes, it's a nice day.

J: **Náho'êhéve'hoohtanôtse oxa'ôheonôtse.** I've come to look at the beaded things.

C: **Naa épêhéva'e, vé'hóóhtôtse!** That's good, look at them!

J: **Eoseepåháva'énôhoonôtse ho'ótanôtse. Néváéso tsémanêstsêstse?** These are really nice chokers. Who made them? (The Preterit mode is used for the first verb to indicate exclamation.)

C: **Hétsêhéóhe he'eo'o Méave'ho'êno émanêstsénovôtse.** Women around here in Lame Deer made them.

J: **Hé'tóhe nápêhévátsésta tséotá'távo. Néváéso tsé-manêstsêstse?** I like this blue one. Who made it?

C: **Nánéehove.** I did.

J: **Ehohtóvåhtovehe.** Is it for sale?

C: **Héehe'e, hé'tóhe émåhehohtóvåhtóvénêstse.** Yes, all of these are for sale.

J: **Etónetoeme?** How much does it (the blue one) cost?

C: **Enévo'oeme.** It's $40.

J: **Epêhéva'e. Nåhtåhohtóva; heta'háanevótse nóhónó'e. Néme'mé'to'enahe?** Good. I'll buy it; here's $50. Do you have change (literally, Can you exchange it?)?

C: **Héehe'e. Nóxa'e, nánêxhéesevéaenanôtse tsétótšêške'oo'êstse.** Yes. Wait, I'll bring back the change.

(There is a slight wait while she gets the change. She returns.)

C: **Heta'háanevótse måhtohto. Mónåhtaéstána hoó'hénóva?** Here's the $10 (change). Shall I put it in a sack?

J: **Héehe'e, hahóo.** Yes, thank you.

C: **Hó'ótóva né'évåhósêho'êhneo'o!** Come back again sometime!

J: **Nåhtsene'évåhósêho'êhne. Hó'ótóva**

nåhtåhohtóvotåhonôtse tsévéstoemo hohpo'eváseehéstotôtse.
I'll come back again. Sometime I'll buy barrettes for my wife.
(Note: barrettes are a fairly recent item for Cheyennes. As
such, a word for 'barrettes' is not well established. We have
checked with a number of speakers and many do not know a word
for 'barrettes.' Some suggest various alternatives. Mrs. Glenmore,
who was quite knowledgeable of terms for grooming, pronounced
this word as hohpo'eáseehéstotôtse (Cheyenne Topical Dictionary,
p. 65). Both authors of this course wish to caution the listener that
there is uncertainty over this word. In contrast, we note, for
interest's sake, that the word for 'braid tie,' me'konáséto, is well
known to many speakers, and this reflects the fact that braid ties
have been used by Cheyennes for a long time.)

C: **Tôhkomo náho'tsenôtse hétsetseha.   Nenóveto háesto
    nåhtsêho'tánêstse.** I have a few now. Shortly I'll have more.
J: **Nêstaévåhósevóomåtse.** I'll see you again.
C: **Héehe'e.** Yes.

Imogene Visits Josephine:
    Next is another visit from Imogene to the home of her friend,
Josephine:

(Imogene comes in the door.)
J: **Vá'ôhtáma.** Welcome. (Literally, (Sit in) the place-of-honor.)
    (Imogene sits down.)
J: **Mónêstsenomêne mo'ôhtávêhohpe?** Will you drink coffee?
I: **Héehe'e, nåhtanomêne.** Yes, I'll drink it.
J: **Naa taomevéståhémahtse!** Well, help yourself!
I: **Héehe'e.** Yes.
(Imogene helps herself to coffee.)
J: **Tósa'e nénêxhé'oohe?** Where did you come from?
I: **Naa namåheóne.** From my house.
J: **Tåxhósé'e néno'kee'e. Naa Aénohe Oxháa'ého'oesêstse?**
    I suppose you're (staying) by yourself again. Where's High
    Hawk (Ted)? (Her husband, Ted, often travels, on tribal
    business.)

I: **Naa étaéšêhósease'háoohe.** Well, he flew away again.

J: **Tósa'e étatšêheše'háoohe?** Where did he fly to?

I: **Naa Vásêtaêno.** To Washington, D.C.

J: **Mónénêhmónetõ'e?** I suppose you just got up.

I: **Naa tóotseha nátó'e.** A LOONG time ago I got up.
(As Josephine designed this conversation, she intended the second word here to have an elongated syllable; usually 'long ago' is pronounced simply as **tótseha.** This elongation of the vowel sound gives emphasis, indicating that Imogene had gotten out of bed a very long time before. There is an element of humor here, also; Josephine was a master of the art of Cheyenne humor.)

J: **Vóóhe néno'ee'êha'onotse?** Did you put your shoes on with the Morning Star? (This is a traditional Cheyenne idiom meaning that one arose very early, when the Morning Star was still up. Here, again, there is humor.)

I: **Hééhe náno'ee'êha'onôtse. Naa Má'háéso?** Of course I put my shoes on with the Morning Star. Where's Old Man (Josephine's husband, Douglas)?

J: **Naa tâxhósé'e héá'e étatsêhe'õhtse Busby K-marts.** Well, I suppose he's gone to the Busby dump again. (Busby residents humorously refer to the town garbage dump as '(Busby) K-Marts,' a take-off on the name of the big general merchandise store, K-Mart, 90 miles west, in Billings, which is frequented by Crow and Cheyenne Indians. At the Busby dump there are often things which have been thrown away which can be rescued or repaired. Here Josephine humorously refers to her husband's penchant for visiting the dump, looking for things that might be usable.)

I: **Naa náametsêhe'õhtse Méave'ho'êno.**
Mónêstsenêhvé'õhtseme? Well, I'm on my way to Lame Deer. Do you want to come with me?

J: **Naa nêstsevé'õhtsemâtse.** I'll go with you.

You Talk Cheyenne, Too?
In the next conversation Wayne Leman and Harry Littlebird
are talking at a powwow in the tribal gym in Lame Deer.

Wayne=W
Harry=H
Mary Fisher=M

H: **Séaa! Kovááhe, mónévésého'éhnéhéhe.** Oh! Youngman
(Wayne), you came here, too.
W: **Héehe'e, náhévé'hóósáne.** Yes, I came to look on.
H: **Hámêstoo'êstse!** Sit down!
(Wayne sits down by Harry. Mary Fisher, sitting nearby,
overhears the conversation, and exclaims to herself:)
M: **Nóoo, vé'ho'e éno'tsêhésenêstéhoo'o!** (The Preterit mode is
used for the verb to indicate exclamation.)
(Wayne overhears Mary and says:)
W: **Héehe'e, nátsêhésenestse tšéške'e. Kovááhe náheševéhe.**
Yes, I talk Cheyenne a little. Youngman is my name.)
M: **Héehe'e, naa hápó'e Ma'heónoó'ôhtá'e náheševéhe.**
Yes, and, likewise, Medicine Corn Woman is my name.
(Mary looks at Wayne's wife, Elena, who has dark hair and an olive
complexion.)
M: **Tsévéstoemôtse éxaenóta'evenóohe.** Your spouse looks like
an Indian woman from another tribe.
W: **Hová'âháne, ésáanótá'évéhe; évé'ho'á'eve.** No, she's not an
Indian woman from another tribe; she's a white woman.
M: **Emo'onahe; étó'êsto'tonohe.** She's pretty; she has long braids.
(Mary notices the young Leman children:)
M: **Móhe tsé'tóhe nenésoneho?** Are these your children?
W: **Héehe'e, nanésoneho.** Yes, (they are) my children.
M: **Enêxoóhtâhéhoono!** They are cute! (Again, the Preterit mode
is used for exclamation. Mrs. Glenmore, who composed this
conversation, suggested that the Cheyenne speaker could not
use the Preterit ending about her (Mary's) own grandchildren,
but here it could be appropriate 'maybe because she never saw
(these children) before.')

W: **Emåheheståhkéveo'o; éto'sevésêho'sóeo'o.** They are all twins (two sets); they are going to take part in the dance.

M: **Naa hápó'e náto'sevésêho'soo'e. Nåhtavéstôhomó'hemoo'o.** And I will dance, likewise. I'll dance with them.

W: **Nápêhévetanóotse tsésto'sevéstôhomó'hémóso nanésoneho.** I'm happy that you're going to dance with my children.

Helping at The Birney Powwow:
The next scene is at a powwow in Birney:

Imogene=I
Josephine=J
Grace Strangeowl=G
Mary=M
Birney ladies=L

I: **Mónêståhéve'hoosenémáne Oévemanåhéno?** Shall we go look on (watch the powwow) at Birney?

J: **Héehe'e, nómôheto.** Yes, let's go.

I: **No'eõhtsêstse netáxe'séestôtse.** Bring along your chair.

J: **Héehe'e naa máto nåhtovéo'kôheo'o naa namotšêške.**
Nåhtsêhexováé'e måhmésêhéto ho'évohkôtse. Yes, and also my umbrella and my knife. I'll cut my meat with it when I eat meat.

I: **Naa amêškévetohko, nêstsevé'šêhóohtanõva.** And a lard bucket, you'll bring home some leftovers. (There is some humor here.)

(They arrive in Birney.)

I: **Tóne'še ééšêho'oésta?** What time is it?

J: **Naa éxaetaeno'kôxe'ohe.** Well, it's exactly 1 o'clock (p.m.).

(They stop at the arbor. No one is around, but there are many cars. People are sitting in the shade at the dance hall.)

J: **Héá'e ééšeáahtse'éene'hanáhtove.** Maybe they've already eaten.

I: **Hová'åháne, héá'e émónêhomôseo'o.** No, maybe they're just now cooking.

(Imogene looks across and sess a big shady lawn area.)

I: **Vé'hoomeha nevá'esêstse. Evové'sáxa ho'évohkôtse.**

Look at that person over there. She's cutting up meat.
(After they sit for awhile:)

J: **Táaxa'e nétåhétsèhetóo'ómáne! Nétåhéve'hoomóneo'o!**
Let's go look! Let's go see them!

I: **Nóheto.** Let's go.
(Imogene grabs her umbrella and starts out.)

I: **Måhvé'ho'soévôtse náto'sèhovéo'kôhomo'he.** If they dance,
I'm gonna do the umbrella dance. (This is quite humorous; there
is no traditional umbrella dance.)
(They go over there and see ladies cutting meat. Stoves are going.)

G: **Nóoo, kåse'éeheho móho'eohtsèhevóhe. Né'ésto'ēhne
néxhéhovéo'oo'e.** Oh, the young ladies (humorous reference to
Imogene and Josephine, who are definitely not young ladies any
more) must have come. Come in and sit in the shade.

M: **Námónèhomôséme. Eno'só'he'konóhta ho'évohkôtse.
Vé'ho'e éxaeno'no'kahe tsévéståhémaétse.** We're just now
cooking. (Part of the extensive humor in this conversation has
to do with the fact that things are running late. Cheyennes joke
about this as 'Indian time.') The meat is still frozen. The
whiteman is the only one who is helping. (This is probably
humorous, also. Mary's husband is a whiteman. Whitemen
sometimes help with cooking, but, apparently, Cheyenne
tradition expects that Indian men will not participate.)

J: **Naa kåhaménèheo'o? Eohkevéståheo'o.** Where are the
committee members? They are (supposed to) help. (The second
word is composed of a noun stem, **kåhaméne**, which is a
modified transliteration of the English word committee, plus the
standard **-o'o** animate plural suffix. Powwow committee
members are obligated to help in the powwow preparations.)

G: **Naa tósa'e he'ho'ôhtsévôtse néhe kåhaménèheo'o!** I don't
know where those committee members could have gone!

I: **Naa táaxa'e na'ěstse motšěške néhmetsèstse.
Nåhtakánomèhósevové'sáxa hé'tohe ho'évohkôtse.**
Well, give me a knife. I'll go ahead and cut up this meat. (The
lateness of the cooking, the fact that the committee members
aren't around to help, and the willingness of the Busby ladies,
who are guests (hence, not expected to work), to help, all these

46

elements add humor to the discourse. Teasing between members of the different reservation districts is common, and some good-natured teasing in action probably occurs in this discourse, as the Busby district ladies offer their services to the Birney district ladies.)

J: **Naa hápó'e na'èstse motšèške néhmetsèstse. Nèstavéståhéotsématsemeno.** And give me a knife, also. We'll help you.

M: **Eno'eáhanenêxåhpónèstse mótšèškehôtse.** The knives are very dull.

(Mary sharpens the knives and gives Imogene and Josephine each one. They start cutting the meat. When they get to the last pan of meat, three or four women arrive.)

I: **Mónêhe'še, nétåhéhovéo'oemãne hátåháóhe hovéo'kôheóne.** Let's go, let's go sit in the shade of the arbor over there.

J: **Nóheto.** Let's go.

(As they leave the cooking area:)

L: **Hahóo, néxaepåhávevéståhéotsémemeno.** Thank you, you helped us well.

In an Elementary School Classroom:

The next scene takes place in an elementary school classroom. There is a bilingual education teacher who speaks Cheyenne.

Teacher=T
3 children=3
Robby=R
Different children=C
John=J
Phillip=P
Annie=A

T: **Ka'èškónêhasèstse, påhávevóonã'o.**

3: **Påhávevóonã'o. Pêhévóonã'o, vovéstomósanéhe. Pêhévevóonã'o.** Good morning. Good morning, teacher. Good morning.

R: **Vovéstomósanéhe, hénová'e tséto'sèhéne'enomátse**

hétsetseha? Teacher, what are we going to study today?

T: **Hétsetseha éšeēva nèstâhéne'anánonèstse tséhešètsèhésevéhése. Néhéne'enanovotse nevéhestovevótse?** Today we will learn what you are named in Cheyenne. Do you know your (Indian) names?

C: **Héehe'e. Héehe'e. Héehe'e. Hová'âháne.** Yes. Yes. Yes. No.

T: **Háahe, Annie, mónésáahéne'enóhe tséhešètsèhésevéheto? Nèstaonésè-hotoo-héne'enánone nonóveto** (many speakers pronounce this word as **nenóveto**). **John, nétónèšètsèhésevéhe?** So, Annie, you don't know your Indian name? We'll try, uh, to learn it shortly. John, what is your Cheyenne name?

J: **Hóma'ke náheševéhe.** My name is Homa'ke.

T: **Epèhéva'e. Naa Phillip, nétónèšètsèhésevéhe?** Good. And Phillip, what is your Indian name?

P: **Naa Netsévóto náheševéhe.** My name is Netsevoto.

T: **Névááso tséno'evéheto?** Who are you named after?

P: **Náno'evéhenôtse tséhešèhéto.** I am named after my maternal uncle.

T: **Robby, nétónèšètsèhésevéhe?** Robby, what is your Indian name?

R: **Naa Ho'évâhtamēhnèstse náheševéhe.** My name is Ho'evâhtamehnèstse. (The name means 'Walking On the Earth.')

T: **Epèhéva'e. Annie, nésáakánomèhéne'enóhe netsèhésevéhestôtse, néhéne'enovohe tséno'evéheto?** Good. Annie, even though you do not know your Indian name, do you know who you are named after?

A: **Héehe'e, náno'evéhenôtse néške'éehe, Mrs.Medicine Elk.** Yes, I am named for my grandmother, Mrs. Medicine Elk.

T: **Héehe, néhéne'enõvo, Vóešèhē'e éheševéhe. Naa hápó'e Vóešèhē'e mónéheševéhehéhe.** Oh, I know her, her (Indian) name is **Voešèhe'e.** So, likewise, you must be **Voešèhe'e.**

A: **Héehe'e, nátaéšèhéne'ēna. Náohkenéstóvo náhko'éehe ôhnèhesèstse.** Yes, I know it now. I have heard my mother saying that.

T: **Hóestanome nemôxe'èstóonéhevótse naa môxe'èstónèstotôtse. Nàhtamôxe'ôhanôtse netsèhésevéhestovevótse naa** néstóoxe'ôhemáhéne. Take out your pieces of paper and pencils. I'll write your Indian names (on the chalkboard) and you copy them.

R: Vovéstomósanéhe, nevá'esêstse mónomáhtsêhéhe namôxe'êstónestôtse. Teacher, someone must have stolen my pencil.

J: Eeeh! Evá'nenêhevoo'o, mónêhvonetanó'tôhéhe hemôxe'êstónestôtse. Hey! He's just saying that, he must have . forgotten (to bring) his pencil.

T: Ho'évåhtamēhnêstse, éohkêhetómêstove. Ho'evåhtamehnêstse, the truth (should) always be (told).

R: Héehe'e, naa nåhtsetónêšemôxe'ôha navéhestôtse? Yes, but how will I write my name?

T: Naahe. Hé'tóhe môxe'êstónestôtse ho'otsêstse hétsetseha. Naa oha né'évataoměho'eotsêstseo'o nemôxe'êstónestôtse måhvóonā'o. Here. Use this pencil now. But bring your own pencil tomorrow.

R: Héehe'e. Yes.

T: Nóheto, nåhtamôxe'ôhanôtse netsêhésevéhestovevótse naa néhmåhetóoxe'ôhemáhéne. Netsévóto, néhvé'ho'énêstsé'tôtse nevéhestôtse. O.K., let's go, I'll write down your Indian names and you all copy them. Netsevoto, say your (Indian)name in English.

P: Naa Eaglefeather. (It's) Eaglefeather. (literally, 'Eagle Tailfeather')

T: Héehe'e, hená'hanehe. Naa Hóma'ke, hénová'e tsénêhestohe tséhvé'ho'énêstsénove? Yes, that's it. Hóma'ke, what does your name mean in English?

R: Naa násáaxaehéne'enóhe. Well, I just don't know.

T: Naa Little Beaver éhenove. Naa Annie, netsêhésevéhestôtse Happy Woman éhenove. Well, it means Little Beaver. And, Annie, your Indian name means Happy Woman.

A: Hahóo. Thank you.

T: Ka'êškónêhasêstse, épêhéva'e tséstaéšêhéne'enomáse nevéhestovevótsenaa tséno'evéhesee'e. Heta'háanehe nevo'êstanéhevêstonane Tséstsêhéståhétse. Hena'háanehe. Children, it's good when you know your (Indian) names and who you are named for. This is our Cheyenne way of life (literally, 'This is the way of life of us Cheyennes.'). That's it ('the end').

A Telephone Conversation:

Ted=T
Wayne=W

(The phone rings at Lemans' house in Hardin, 40 miles west of Busby, where Ted lives:)

T: **Kovááhe? Youngman?**

W: **Héehe'e, nánéehove.** Yes, this is me.

T: **Nánéehove Aénohe Oxháa'ého'oesêstse.** This is High Hawk.

W: **Héehe'e.** Yes.

T: **Nénêsto'sêtsêhe'oohehe Vóhpoométanéno hétsetseha éšeẽva?** Are you going to come to Busby today?

W: **Héehe'e, nåhtaonåháxêho'eohe, náhešêtano. Néhotse'óhetanohe?** Yes, I might come, I've been thinking. Do you want to work?

T: **Ma'énêsétovoésta náme'hotse'ohe. Náto'sêhestometsêhe'õhtse Mo'õhtávôheomenéno hétsetseha tséhvóonã'o.** After noon I can work. I have to go to a meeting in Lame Deer this morning.

W: **Epêhéva'e, nåhtåho'eohe ma'taéšemésêhéto.** Good, I'll come after I eat.

T: **Etónêšeéšeeve nåháóhe?** What kind of a day is it over there? (What's the weather like over there?)

W: **Ehoo'kõho.** It's raining.

T: **Hétsêhéno éasêho'ééto.** Around here it's starting to snow.

W: **Nåhtanôhtsevóómo Vó'keme ma'taameohéto!** I'll look for Old Man Winter as I travel along!

T: **Héehe'e, kahkêse nêstavóomåtse.** Yes, I'll see you soon.

Husband and Wife Fixing Drymeat:

Next is a conversation between a couple in their home.

Imogene=I
Ted=T

I: **Aénohe Oxháa'ého'oesêstse, nénaóotsehe?** High Hawk, are
you sleeping?

T: **Hová'åháne, nává'nêhosotóméše.** No, I'm just resting.

I: **Hé'tóhe motšêške énêxáhpo, néxhéehãhtsêstse!**
Náto'sema'xeó'êsóva. This knife is dull, come sharpen it! I'm
going to make a lot of drymeat.

T: **Eto'setónêšévenove?** What's going to be happening?

I: **Ma'tåhósema'heóneéšeeve éto'seévaonóomeo'o**
Vóestaa'e hevo'êstanemo. Next Sunday there will be a
call-back for the family of White Buffalo Woman (Josephine
Glenmore).

T: **Héehe'e, étaéšeno'keaénoo'e tséhe'šêhovánee'êse.**
Oh, yes, it's been one year since she has been gone (died).

I: **Héehe'e, náohkêsó'hoháehoónôsé'ota. Hó'ótóva**
náohkêsó'hésta'xanenôtse Vóestaa'e. Yes, I still miss her very
much. Sometimes I still cry for Josephine.

T: **Tósa'e néhéstána héne ho'évohkôtse?** Where did you get that
meat?

I: **Naa Mó'ôhno'keóó'êstse mótó'omemåsôhevóhe váotseváhne**
háne éšeeva. Hevésenóho móvéståhémaehevóhe tsé'óénôse.
Ma'xêhotóaváótséva éhoháahpē'o ho'évohkôtse. Well, (my
son) Elk Stands Alone shot a deer yesterday. His friend helped
him skin it. (It must have been) a big buck, there sure is a lot of
meat.

T: **Epêhéva'e, tåxo'e tsêhoháetanevóo'e ma'évaonóomêvôtse.**
Naa hotoo éehaseo'o? That's good, there will probably be lots
of people at the call-back. Where's, uh, the sharpener?

I: **Nêhéóhe a'e ho'êstáva éhoo'e.** There it is next to the stove.

T: **Nátaéševóóhta. Néhmetsêstse motšêške!** I see it now. Give
me the knife!

I: **Naahe.** Here.

T: **Tósa'e néto'seó'ěsóva?** Where are you going to slice the meat?

I: **Hétsěhéóhe nahe. Hoóxé'e éhoésenao'o. Naa máto séhpató'ôheonôtse ého'táněstse.** Right here (in the kitchen). The poles are hanging. And also the (meat) stretching pins are (here).

Giving a Ride on the Way To Church:

The next conversation takes place when a grandfather and his grandson help a lady by giving her a ride to church.

Ted=T
Phillip=P
Gladys=G

T: **Néxahe, Hotóhpěhéévá'e nea'háanehe tsétaameõhtsěstse. Taéneohévoo'o.** Grandson, that's Buffalo Rope Woman walking. Stop driving (when you get to her).

P: **Héehe'e, náměšeme.** Yes, grandfather.

(They stop. Ted rolls down the window and speaks:)

T: **Hotóhpěhéévá'e, tósa'e ného'ôhtse?** Buffalo Rope Woman, where are you going?

G: **Naa nátatsěhe'ôhtse ma'heóneéestsémåheóne.** I'm going to the church.

T: **Hápó'e nahe, nåháóhe nátsěhe'ôhtséme. Táxevonēhněstse!** Likewise us, we are going there. Get on!

G: **Hahóo. Hestóxemé'one nåhtåhoo'e. Nóoo, éxahe móéšeáahtse'nôhtóva'éno'haměhéhe!** Thank you. I'll get in the back. Oh my, your grandson knows how to drive already!

T: **Héehe'e, návovéstomévo nonóhpa nåhtsene'ôhkeama'éno'-hamotaha.** Yes, I taught him so that he could drive for me.

G: **Epěhéva'éneho!** That's good! (Preterit mode.)

T: **Hénáá'e ho'éva tséhéseaměhneto?** Why are you walking? (Literally, 'Why on the ground are you going along?')

G: **Naamåho'hestôtse éonéněšeotse.** My car broke down.

T: **Etóněsóotse?** What happened?

G: **Ho'ēsta mónaeotsėhéhe.** I guess the battery (literally, 'fire') died.

T: **Néto'sėhohtóvanotse tsémónaestse?** Are you going to buy a new one?

G: **Ema'xėhótoanáto; násáahema'kaetaeméhe hétsetseha násáanóhpatónėšėhohtóvåhenôtse tsémónaestse.** It's really difficult; I don't have money now so I can't buy a new one.

T: **Etónetoemeo'o?** How much do they cost?

G: **Héá'ėháma naesóhtóhnó'e ma'kaeta.** Maybe $60.

T: **Tóne'še néto'sėhósėho'eonénėxôhemõne?** When will you get your next check?

G: **Naa tsenėxho'táhó'ta môxe'ėstóoné-amó'eneóne na'ha naa máto neva ma'éšeeve. Nėhe'še nåhtåhohtóvanôtse tsémónaestse.** Well, it should be on the mail truck on Wednesday or Thursday. Then I'll buy a new (battery).

T: **Epėhéva'e. Naa måhvé'tsėhe'oohétanoto hohtóvamåheóne naa máto Mo'ôhtávôheomenéno néhvá'neéestsėstáootsé'- tovemenoo'o naa nėstatsėhe'oohé'tovatséme.** That's good. And if you want to go to the store or Lame Deer just call us and we'll take you there. (The extra **tšėheše-** heard on the tape in the word beginning **måhvé-** is a false start. Mr. Risingsun wishes the verb to be as it is typed here.)

G: **Hahóo.** Thank you.

T: **Naa nééšėho'eohémáne ma'heóneéestsémåheóne. Anóse onésenoohtomeo'o tséamo'xeto.** Well, we have arrived at the church. Try to leave your load outside (the door).

(On tape the second sentence begins with **Onésė-hotoo-anóse-noohtomeo'o.** During checking of this tape, Mr. Risingsun wished the Cheyenne to be changed to the proper order, as given above. The 'word' **hotoo** heard during the taped sequence here is the Cheyenne way of indicating hesitation or uncertainty, equivalent to English 'uh.' If you wish to become a better speaker of Cheyenne, learn to say **hotoo,** instead of 'uh,' if you reach a point of uncertainty in your speech. We have allowed the one or two other taped instances of hotoo to remain in the typed transcription of the tapes, to show how a fluent speaker of the language has used this hesitation marker.

Ordinarily, for polished publication, these hesitation 'words' would be edited out, according to the wishes of the Cheyenne speakers.)

G: **Héehe'e, é'ôhkenêhevoo'o Háá'êše Oxhasêstse. Naa 'Nêstsevé'eévâhósêhestanánóvo neamo'xéstóvévo,' é'ôhkêhevoo'o.** Yes, that's what Travels From Afar (Rev. Habegger) used to say. And, 'Don't take up your burden again,' he used to say.

T: **Héehe'e, náohkenéstomónenôtse, é'ôhkenêhesêstse. Nétaéstsêhnema!** Yes, I've heard of him (that) he used to say that. Let's go inside!

At a Church Meal in Lame Deer:

Joe=J
Victoria=V
Wayne=W
Regina=R
Sylvester=S

J: **Haaahe.** Hello.
W: **Haaahe.** Hello.
J: **Néháeanahe?** Are you hungry?
W: **Héehe'e, náoseeháéána.** Yes, I'm very hungry.
J: **Naa éme'vovóehnénove nonóhpa nêstanéhemésehe.** Well, you should be first in line so you can eat soon.

(Now, speaking in a louder voice to the people gathered:)

J: **Epêhéva'e tséhmâheho'êhnése hétsetseha hetóéva. Naa he'eo'o étaéšeéxaneneo'otsésto'sêhoxotávôse. Vó'kaa'e Ohvovó'haestse, néxháóénâtse!** It's good that you all came this evening. The women are ready to serve the food now. Spotted Antelope, pray (please)!

S: **Naa Ma'hêõ'o he'ama tséhestoéstoveto, néháoena'tovatsemeno. Hahóo néhetatsemeno tséhešemano'ée'tovatsemenoto tséhéóhe. Néstáxêhe'oná'o'tovemeno nâhtsevé'šêpêhévomóhtâhénone hé'tóhe mésêhestôtse, nâhtsevé'sêhetótaetanónóne naa tsésto'semóheeohtsétse néssóhpeéestsêstsé'toveha nêstotse'ono. Hahóo**

névé'šêhetatsemeno nee'ha hevéhéstóva, Jesus. Nêhe'še.
God, you who dwell above (in heaven), we pray to you. 'Thank
you,' we say to you, that we are meeting together with you here.
Put your hand on us so that we will feel good from this food,
(and) that we will be joyful. And when we have our meeting,
speak through your servants (workers). 'Thank you,' we say
through the name of your son, Jesus. The end (Amen).

V: **Tsea'háanehe nêhe'onáxestôtse, naa háméško, naa
ane'kôheo'o, naa motšêške.** Here's a napkin, and spoon, and
fork, and knife.

W: **Hahóo.** Thank you.

R: **Heta'háanéhe néstáme. Ného'åhehe vétšêškévåhonoo'o?**
Here's your food. Do you want frybread?

W: **Héehe'e, náohkepêhévé'áhta.** Yes, I like its taste.

R: **Héá'e nétaéšêto'sêtsêhéstahe.** Maybe you are almost a
Cheyenne.

W: **Héá'êháma.** Maybe so.

(Wayne sees Sylvester and greets him:)

W: **Vó'kaa'e Ohvovó'haestse, haahe.** Hello, Spotted Antelope.

S: **Haaahe.** Hello.

W: **Mónêstanéšeema?** Shall we sit together?

S: **Héehe'e.** Yes.

W: **Né'asêtanôtse vóhpoma'ôhtse naa ménemenôtse!**
Pass the salt and pepper!'

S: **Naa hápó'e né'asêtanôtse vé'keemahpe!** And, likewise, pass
the sugar!

W: **Tá'sótse néohkêsáaméséhe vé'keemahpe tséhvé'keemåhpévomóhtåheto.** I thought you don't eat sugar
because you have diabetes (literally, sugar-sickness').

S: **Naa náohkêsáaho'åhéhe hé'tóhe aéstomevé'keemahpe.
Tšéške'e vé'keemahpe mónáme'héonêxanaa'e.**
Well, I don't like this artificial sugar. A little sugar surely won't
hurt me.

W: **Hé'tóhe ho'évohkôtse éoseepêhévéeno'e.** This meat sure tastes
good.

S: **Eno'he'ke. Mónôhtóvåhá'enêhevóhe tséhomôsese.**
It's also tender. The cooks know how to cook.

Review (not on tape):

You have probably learned more than you realize by now. Try to see how many of the following Cheyenne words and phrases you recognize. When learning a language, it is, of course, best to practice so much that you begin thinking in that language. So, if you can think of the meanings of the following words without translating to English, that is best. But, for many of us, we will still find it helpful to review, even by translating to English. Have fun!

Etonéto.
Nétónêševéhe?
Náháéána.
Tósa'e néhoo'e?
ho'évohkôtse
náhko'éehe
ného'éehe
néške'e
néséne
Néá'eše.
héehe'e
Epêhéva'e.
Estséhnêstse!
Hámêstoo'êstse!
He'kotoo'êstse!
Néóxôheve?
Hósenêhešeha!
Nétâhéve'hoosanema!
Nétâhéo'enemenama!
hẽ'e
hetane
Ma'hẽõ'o
Eonénêšeotse
Néhmetsêstse!

vé'ho'e
mo'éhno'ha
Népêhévatsêstahe?
Nápêhévátsésta.
Náho'ahe.
Nékåhaneotsehe?
Nákåhaneotse.
Névóomohe?
Návóómo.
Nétaéšêhéne'enahe?
Nátaéšêhéne'ẽna.
Násáahéne'enóhe.
Tósa'e ného'õhtse?
Tóne'še néévåho'êhóó'óhtse?
Ešeẽva náévåho'êhóó'óhtse.
Naa eho?
Ehotse'ohe.
Névááhe?
Tóne'še ého'oésta?
Hénáá'e tsého'åheto?
Nétsêhésenêstsehe?
Nátšêške'tsêhésenestse.
Néstsêhésenêstovêstse!
Né'asêtanôtse vóhpoma'ôhtse!

56

Notes:

Other Cheyenne Language Books:

You might find it helpful to purchase a Cheyenne dictionary or grammar book. The English-Cheyenne Student Dictionary was published in 1976 and is currently available for $14.95 (plus $1.00 postage for single copies; there is no postage charge when more than one copy is ordered) from:

> Montana Council for Indian Education
> Box 31215
> Billings, Montana 59107

A larger dictionary was published in 1984 with the title Cheyenne Topical Dictionary, by Josephine Stands In Timber and Wayne Leman. It is available for $18.00 (plus $2.00 postage) from:

> CCEP
> Box 50
> Busby, MT 59016

Both dictionaries may also be available from the bookstore at Dull Knife Memorial College, Lame Deer, Montana 59043. You may check with the bookstore by calling the college office at (406) 477-6215, and asking for the bookstore extension, to see if these dictionaries are in stock.

A grammar book was published in 1980 (sometimes listed as 1979), with the title, A Reference Grammar of the Cheyenne Language. Contact CCEP at the address given above in Busby, Montana, or call CCEP at (406) 592-3643, if you are interested in purchasing a grammar book (or dictionary). CCEP also has available for sale many other Cheyenne materials including calendars, spiritual song tapes, a church hymnbook, history and story books (in Cheyenne with English translations), and translations of the Cheyenne Bible. A form for ordering Cheyenne language materials from CCEP is available free from CCEP. Just call or write for the order form.

About the authors:

Mr. Ted Risingsun, the Cheyenne speaker on these tapes, was a Cheyenne elder, a tribal leader, and the great grandson of the Cheyenne leader Dull Knife. He frequently served as an elected member of the Northern Cheyenne Tribal Council, and often represented his tribe at official meetings in Washington, D.C., and elsewhere. Born in 1926, Mr. Risingsun attended the B.I.A.boarding school in Busby, MT, then known as the Tongue River Boarding School. He took high school and post-high school education at schools in Kansas and South Dakota. He had a distinguished career serving with the U.S. Army in World War II and the Korean War. In 1972, Mr. Risingsun became the first director of the Federally-funded Title VII Bilingual Education Program on the Northern Cheyenne Reservation. He believed strongly that the Cheyenne language is a vital component of Cheyenne culture, and worked with programs to maintain the Cheyenne language and culture. He died in 1995.

Mr. Wayne Leman was born in 1949, in Alaska. He attended elementary and high school in the small fishing village of Ninilchik. His family, of Russian-Aleut ancestry of that area of Alaska, continues the commercial salmon fishing trade that he grew up with from childhood. He attended schools in Chicago, Kansas, and Oregon, majoring in linguistics. In 1975, he and his wife, Elena, moved to the Northern Cheyenne Reservation at the invitation of tribal church leaders to assist churches on the reservation, as well as all the Cheyenne people of Montana and Oklahoma, in Cheyenne language materials development.

For many years, Mr. Leman's primary co-worker was Mrs. Josephine Glenmore. A deep relationship of academic respect and affection developed during the many hours of work and other community associations Mrs. Glenmore and the Lemans shared. It is with grief, yet sincere gratefulness, that we dedicate this language learning course to the memory of Mrs. Glenmore. She was a fine teacher and a dear friend.